Usborne
Illustrated Originals

EDWARD LEAR'S

BOOK OF NONSENSE

Usborne
Illustrated Originals

EDWARD LEAR'S

BOOK OF NONSENSE

ILLUSTRATED BY CHRISTINE PYM

CONTENTS

LIMERICKS

There was an Old Man with a nose,
Who said, "If you choose to suppose
That my nose is too long,
You are certainly wrong!"
That remarkable Man with a nose.

There was an Old Man of the Hague,
Whose ideas were excessively vague;
He built a balloon,
To examine the moon,
That deluded Old Man of the Hague.

There was an Old Man of Moldavia,
Who had the most curious behaviour;
For while he was able,
He slept on a table,
That funny Old Man of Moldavia.

There was an Old Man of Peru,
Who never knew what he should do;
So he tore off his hair,
And behaved like a bear,
That intrinsic Old Man of Peru.

12

There was an Old Man with a beard,
Who said, "It is just as I feared! –
Two owls and a hen,
Four larks and a wren,
Have all built their nests in my beard!"

There was a Young Lady of Ryde,
Whose shoe-strings were seldom untied.
She purchased some clogs,
And some small spotted dogs,
And frequently walked about Ryde.

There was a Young Lady whose chin
Resembled the point of a pin;
So she had it made sharp,
And purchased a harp,
And played several tunes with her chin.

There was an Old Person of Dutton,
Whose head was as small as a button;
So, to make it look big,
He purchased a wig,
And rapidly rushed about Dutton.

There was a Young Lady whose eyes
Were unique as to colour and size;
When she opened them wide,
People all turned aside,
And started away in surprise.

18

There was an Old Person of Woking,
Whose mind was perverse and provoking;
He sat on a rail,
With his head in a pail,
That illusive Old Person of Woking.

There was a Young Lady of Turkey,
Who wept when the weather was murky;
When the day turned out fine,
She ceased to repine,
That capricious Young Lady of Turkey.

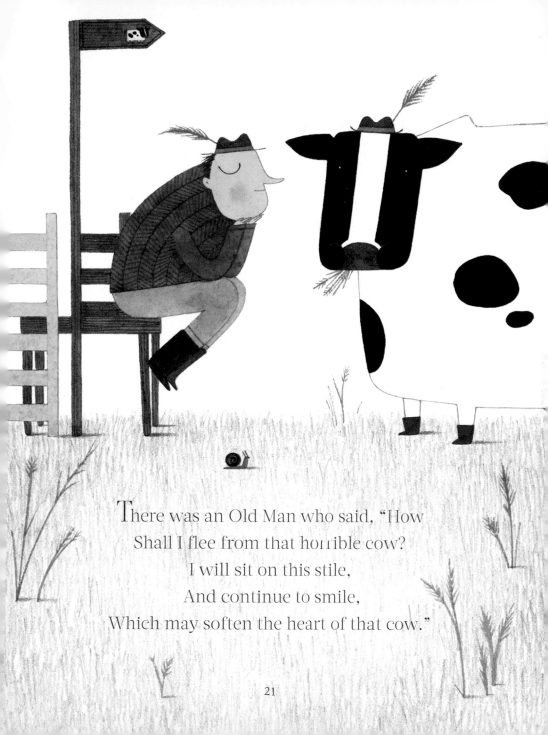

There was an Old Man who said, "How
Shall I flee from that horrible cow?
I will sit on this stile,
And continue to smile,
Which may soften the heart of that cow."

There was an Old Man of the coast,
Who placidly sat on a post;
But when it was cold,
He relinquished his hold,
And called for some hot-buttered toast.

There was a Young Lady of Bute,
Who played on a silver-gilt flute;
She played several jigs,
To her uncle's white pigs, –
That amusing Young Lady of Bute.

There was an Old Person of Slough,
Who danced at the end of a bough;
But they said, "If you sneeze,
You might damage the trees,
You imprudent Old Person of Slough."

There was an Old Lady of Chertsey,
Who made a remarkable curtsey;
She twirled round and round,
Till she sank underground,
Which distressed all the people of Chertsey.

There was an Old Person of Ware,
Who rode on the back of a bear:
When they'd ask'd, "Does it trot?" –
He said, "Certainly not!
He's a Moppsikon Floppsikon bear!"

There was an Old Man on the Border,
Who lived in the utmost disorder;
He danced with the cat,
And made tea in his hat,
Which vexed all the folks on the Border.

There was an Old Man in a boat,
Who said, "I'm afloat! I'm afloat!"
When they said, "No, you ain't!"
He was ready to faint,
That unhappy Old Man in a boat.

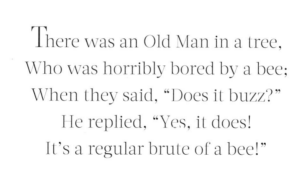

There was an Old Man in a tree,
Who was horribly bored by a bee;
When they said, "Does it buzz?"
He replied, "Yes, it does!
It's a regular brute of a bee!"

NONSENSE
SONGS

THE OWL AND THE PUSSY-CAT

I.

The Owl and the Pussy-Cat went to sea
In a beautiful pea-green boat,
They took some honey, and plenty of money,
Wrapped up in a five-pound note.
The Owl looked up to the stars above,
And sang to a small guitar,
"O lovely Pussy! O Pussy, my love,
What a beautiful Pussy you are,
You are,
You are!
What a beautiful Pussy you are!"

II.

Pussy said to the Owl, "You elegant fowl!
How charmingly sweet you sing!
O let us be married! too long we have tarried:
But what shall we do for a ring?"
They sailed away, for a year and a day,
To the land where the Bong-tree grows,
And there in a wood a Piggy-wig stood
With a ring at the end of his nose,
His nose,
His nose,
With a ring at the end of his nose.

III.

"Dear Pig, are you willing to sell for one shilling
Your ring?" Said the Piggy, "I will."
So they took it away, and were married next day
By the Turkey who lives on the hill.
They dinèd on mince, and slices of quince,
Which they ate with a runcible spoon;

And hand in hand, on the edge of the sand,
They danced by the light of the moon,
The moon,
The moon,
They danced by the light of the moon.

THE JUMBLIES

I.

They went to sea in a Sieve, they did,
In a Sieve they went to sea:
In spite of all their friends could say,
On a winter's morn, on a stormy day,
In a Sieve they went to sea!
And when the Sieve turned round and round,
And every one cried, "You'll all be drowned!"
They called aloud, "Our Sieve ain't big,
But we don't care a button! we don't care a fig!
In a Sieve we'll go to sea!"
Far and few, far and few,
Are the lands where the Jumblies live;
Their heads are green, and their hands are blue,
And they went to sea in a Sieve.

II.

They sailed away in a Sieve, they did,
In a Sieve they sailed so fast,
With only a beautiful pea-green veil
Tied with a riband by way of a sail,
To a small tobacco-pipe mast;
And every one said, who saw them go,
"O won't they be soon upset, you know!
For the sky is dark, and the voyage is long,
And happen what may, it's extremely wrong
In a Sieve to sail so fast!"
Far and few, far and few,
Are the lands where the Jumblies live;
Their heads are green, and their hands are blue,
And they went to sea in a Sieve.

III.

The water it soon came in, it did,
The water it soon came in;
So to keep them dry, they wrapped their feet
In a pinky paper all folded neat,
And they fastened it down with a pin.
And they passed the night in a crockery-jar,
And each of them said, "How wise we are!
Though the sky be dark, and the voyage be long,
Yet we never can think we were rash or wrong,
While round in our Sieve we spin!"
Far and few, far and few,
Are the lands where the Jumblies live;
Their heads are green, their hands are blue,
And they went to sea in a Sieve.

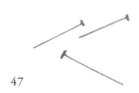

IV.

And all night long they sailed away;
And when the sun went down,
They whistled and warbled a moony song
To the echoing sound of a coppery gong,
In the shade of the mountains brown.
"O Timballo! How happy we are,
When we live in a sieve and a crockery-jar,
And all night long in the moonlight pale,
We sail away with a pea-green sail,
In the shade of the mountains brown!"
Far and few, far and few,
Are the lands where the Jumblies live;
Their heads are green, and their hands are blue
And they went to sea in a Sieve.

V.

They sailed to the Western Sea, they did,
To a land all covered with trees,
And they brought an Owl, and a useful Cart,
And a pound of Rice, and a Cranberry Tart,
And a hive of silvery Bees,
And they brought a Pig, and some green Jack-daws,
And a lovely Monkey with lollipop paws,
And forty bottles of Ring-Bo-Ree,
And no end of Stilton Cheese.
Far and few, far and few,
Are the lands where the Jumblies live;
Their heads are green, and their hands are blue,
And they went to sea in a Sieve.

VI.

And in twenty years they all came back,
In twenty years or more,
And every one said, "How tall they've grown!
For they've been to the Lakes, the Torrible Zone,
And the hills of the Chankly Bore!"
And they drank their health, and gave them a feast
Of dumplings made of beautiful yeast;
And every one said, "If only we live,
We too will go to sea in a Sieve, –
To the hills of the Chankly Bore!"
Far and few, far and few,
Are the lands where the Jumblies live;
Their heads are green and their hands are blue,
And they went to sea in a Sieve.

THE NUTCRACKERS AND THE SUGAR-TONGS

I.

The Nutcrackers sat by a plate on the table,
The Sugar-tongs sat by a plate at his side;
And the Nutcrackers said,
"Don't you wish we were able
Along the blue hills and green meadows to ride?
Must we drag on this stupid existence for ever,
So idle and weary so full of remorse, –
While every one else takes his pleasure and never
Seems happy unless he is riding a horse?"

II.

"Don't you think we could ride without being instructed?
Without any saddle, or bridle, or spur?
Our legs are so long, and so aptly constructed,
I'm sure that an accident could not occur.
Let us all of a sudden hop down from the table,
And hustle downstairs, and each jump on a horse!
Shall we try? Shall we go? Do you think we are able?"
The Sugar-tongs answered distinctly, "Of course!"

III.

So down the long staircase they hopped in a minute,
The Sugar-tongs snapped, and the Crackers said "Crack!"
The stable was open, the horses were in it;
Each took out a pony, and jumped on his back.
The Cat in a fright scrambled out of the doorway,
The Mice tumbled out of a bundle of hay,
The brown and white Rats, and the black ones from Norway,
Screamed out, "They are taking the horses away!"

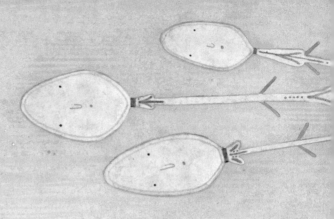

IV.

The whole of the household was filled with amazement,
The Cups and the Saucers danced madly about,
The Plates and the Dishes looked out of the casement,
The Saltcellar stood on his head with a shout,
The Spoons with a clatter looked out of the lattice,
The Mustard-pot climbed up the Gooseberry Pies,
The Soup-ladle peeped through a heap of Veal Patties,
And squeaked with a ladle-like scream of surprise.

V.

The Frying-pan said, "It's an awful delusion!"
The Tea-kettle hissed and grew black in the face;
And they all rushed downstairs in the wildest confusion,
To see the great Nutcracker-Sugar-tong race.
And out of the stable, with screamings and laughter,
(Their ponies were cream-coloured, speckled with brown),
The Nutcrackers first, and the Sugar-tongs after,
Rode all round the yard, and then all round the town.

VI.

They rode through the street, and they rode by the station,
They galloped away to the beautiful shore;
In silence they rode, and "made no observation,"
Save this: "We will never go back any more!"
And still you might hear, till they rode out of hearing,
The Sugar-tongs snap, and the Crackers say "Crack!"
Till far in the distance their forms disappearing,
They faded away. – And they never came back!

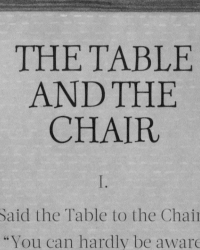

THE TABLE
AND THE
CHAIR

I.

Said the Table to the Chair,
"You can hardly be aware
How I suffer from the heat,
And from chilblains on my feet!
If we took a little walk,
We might have a little talk!
Pray let us take the air!"
Said the Table to the Chair.

II.

Said the Chair unto the Table,
"Now you *know* we are not able!
How foolishly you talk,
When you know we *cannot* walk!"
Said the Table, with a sigh,
"It can do no harm to try,
I've as many legs as you,
Why can't we walk on two?"

III.

So they both went slowly down,
And walked about the town
With a cheerful bumpy sound,
As they toddled round and round.
And everybody cried,
As they hastened to their side,
"See! the Table and the Chair
Have come out to take the air!"

IV.

But in going down an alley,
To a castle in the valley,
They completely lost their way,
And wandered all the day,
Till, to see them safely back.
They paid a Ducky-quack,
And a Beetle, and a Mouse,
Who took them to their house.

V.

Then they whispered to each other,
    "O delightful little brother!
What a lovely walk we've taken!
Let us dine on Beans and Bacon!"
So the Ducky and the leetle
Browny-Mousy and the Beetle
Dined, and danced upon their heads
Till they toddled to their beds.

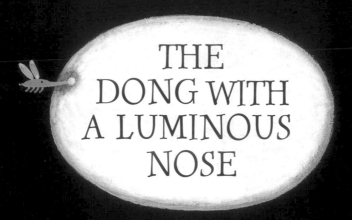

THE
DONG WITH
A LUMINOUS
NOSE

When awful darkness and silence reign
Over the great Gromboolian plain,
Through the long, long wintry nights; –
When the angry breakers roar
As they beat on the rocky shore; –
When Storm-clouds brood on the towering heights
Of the Hills of the Chankly Bore: –

Then, through the vast and gloomy dark,
There moves what seems a fiery spark,
A lonely spark with silvery rays
Piercing the coal-black night, –
A Meteor strange and bright: –
Hither and thither the vision strays,
A single lurid light.

Slowly it wanders, – pauses, – creeps, –
Anon it sparkles, – flashes and leaps;
And ever as onward it gleaming goes
A light on the Bong-tree stems it throws.
And those who watch at that midnight hour
From Hall or Terrace, or lofty Tower,
Cry, as the wild light passes along, –
"The Dong! – the Dong!
The wandering Dong through the forest goes!
The Dong! the Dong!
The Dong with a luminous Nose!"

Long years ago
The Dong was happy and gay,
Till he fell in love with a Jumbly Girl
Who came to those shores one day.
For the Jumblies came in a sieve, they did, –
Landing at eve near the Zemmery Fidd
Where the Oblong Oysters grow,
And the rocks are smooth and gray.
And all the woods and the valleys rang
With the Chorus they daily and nightly sang, –
"Far and few, far and few,
Are the lands where the Jumblies live;
Their heads are green, and their hands are blue,
And they went to sea in a sieve."

74

Happily, happily passed those days!
While the cheerful Jumblies staid;
They danced in circlets all night long,
To the plaintive pipe of the lively Dong,
In the moonlight, shine, or shade.
For day and night he was always there
By the side of the Jumbly Girl so fair,
With her sky-blue hands, and her sea-green hair,
Till the morning came of that hateful day
When the Jumblies sailed in their sieve away,

And the Dong was left on the cruel shore
Gazing – gazing for evermore, –
Ever keeping his weary eyes on
That pea-green sail on the far horizon, –
Singing the Jumbly Chorus still
As he sat all day on the grassy hill, –
"Far and few, far and few,
Are the lands where the Jumblies live;
Their heads are green, and their hands are blue,
And they went to sea in a sieve."

But when the sun was low in the West,
The Dong arose and said; –
"What little sense I once possessed
Has quite gone out of my head!" –
And since that day he wanders still
By lake and forest, marsh and hill,
Singing – "O somewhere, in valley or plain
Might I find my Jumbly Girl again!
For ever I'll seek by lake and shore
Till I find my Jumbly Girl once more!"

Playing a pipe with silvery squeaks,
Since then his Jumbly Girl he seeks,
And because by night he could not see,
He gathered the bark of the Twangum Tree
On the flowery plain that grows.
And he wove him a wondrous Nose, –
A Nose as strange as a Nose could be!
Of vast proportions and painted red,
And tied with cords to the back of his head.
– In a hollow rounded space it ended
With a luminous lamp within suspended,
All fenced about
With a bandage stout
To prevent the wind from blowing it out; –
And with holes all round to send the light,
In gleaming rays on the dismal night.

And now each night, and all night long,
Over those plains still roams the Dong;
And above the wail of the Chimp and Snipe
You may hear the squeak of his plaintive pipe
While ever he seeks, but seeks in vain
To meet with his Jumbly Girl again;
Lonely and wild – all night he goes, –
The Dong with a luminous Nose!
And all who watch at the midnight hour,
From Hall or Terrace, or lofty Tower,
Cry, as they trace the Meteor bright,
Moving along through the dreary night, –
"This is the hour when forth he goes,
The Dong with a luminous Nose!
Yonder – over the plain he goes;
He goes!
He goes;
The Dong with a luminous Nose!"

THE COURTSHIP OF THE YONGHY-BONGHY-BÒ

I.

On the Coast of Coromandel
Where the early pumpkins blow,
In the middle of the woods
Lived the Yonghy-Bonghy-Bò.
Two old chairs, and half a candle, –
One old jug without a handle, –
These were all his worldly goods:
In the middle of the woods,
These were all the worldly goods,
Of the Yonghy-Bonghy-Bò,
Of the Yonghy-Bonghy-Bò.

II.

Once, among the Bong-trees walking
Where the early pumpkins blow,
To a little heap of stones
Came the Yonghy-Bonghy-Bò.
There he heard a Lady talking,
To some milk-white Hens of Dorking, –
"'Tis the Lady Jingly Jones!
On that little heap of stones
Sits the Lady Jingly Jones!"
Said the Yonghy-Bonghy-Bò,
Said the Yonghy-Bonghy-Bò.

III.

"Lady Jingly! Lady Jingly!
Sitting where the pumpkins blow,
Will you come and be my wife?"
Said the Yonghy-Bonghy-Bò.
"I am tired of living singly, –
On this coast so wild and shingly, –
I'm a-weary of my life;
If you'll come and be my wife,
Quite serene would be my life!" –
Said the Yonghy-Bonghy-Bò,
Said the Yonghy-Bonghy-Bò.

IV.

"On this Coast of Coromandel,
Shrimps and watercresses grow,
Prawns are plentiful and cheap,"
Said the Yonghy-Bonghy-Bò.
"You shall have my Chairs and candle,
And my jug without a handle! –
Gaze upon the rolling deep
(Fish is plentiful and cheap;)
As the sea, my love is deep!"
Said the Yonghy-Bonghy-Bò,
Said the Yonghy-Bonghy-Bò.

V.

Lady Jingly answered sadly,
And her tears began to flow, –
"Your proposal comes too late,
    Mr. Yonghy-Bonghy-Bò!
I would be your wife most gladly!"
(Here she twirled her fingers madly,)
"But in England I've a mate,
Yes! you've asked me far too late,
For in England I've a mate,
    Mr. Yonghy-Bonghy-Bò!
    Mr. Yonghy-Bonghy-Bò!"

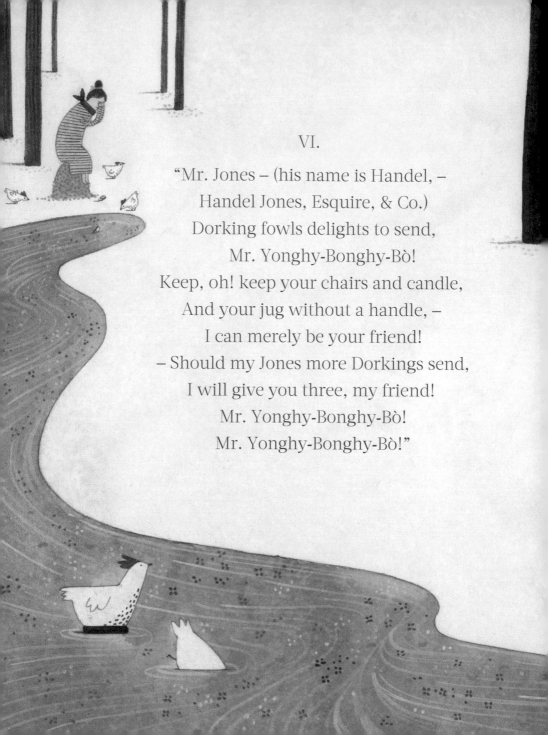

VI.

"Mr. Jones – (his name is Handel, –
Handel Jones, Esquire, & Co.)
Dorking fowls delights to send,
Mr. Yonghy-Bonghy-Bò!
Keep, oh! keep your chairs and candle,
And your jug without a handle, –
I can merely be your friend!
– Should my Jones more Dorkings send,
I will give you three, my friend!
Mr. Yonghy-Bonghy-Bò!
Mr. Yonghy-Bonghy-Bò!"

VII.

"Though you've such a tiny body,
And your head so large doth grow, –
Though your hat may blow away,
Mr. Yonghy-Bonghy-Bò!
Though you're such a Hoddy Doddy –
Yet I wish that I could modi-
fy the words I needs must say!
Will you please to go away?
That is all I have to say –
Mr. Yonghy-Bonghy-Bò!
Mr. Yonghy-Bonghy-Bò!"

VIII.

Down the slippery slopes of Myrtle,
Where the early pumpkins blow,
To the calm and silent sea
Fled the Yonghy-Bonghy-Bò.
There, beyond the Bay of Gurtle,
Lay a large and lively Turtle; –
"You're the Cove," he said, "for me
On your back beyond the sea,
Turtle, you shall carry me!"
Said the Yonghy-Bonghy-Bò,
Said the Yonghy-Bonghy-Bò.

IX.

Through the silent-roaring ocean
Did the Turtle swiftly go;
Holding fast upon his shell
Rode the Yonghy-Bonghy-Bò.
With a sad primæval motion
Towards the sunset isles of Boshen
Still the Turtle bore him well.
Holding fast upon his shell,
"Lady Jingly Jones, farewell!"
Sang the Yonghy-Bonghy-Bò,
Sang the Yonghy-Bonghy-Bò.

X.

From the Coast of Coromandel,
Did that Lady never go;
On that heap of stones she mourns
For the Yonghy-Bonghy-Bò.
On that Coast of Coromandel,
In his jug without a handle,
Still she weeps, and daily moans;
On that little heap of stones
To her Dorking Hens she moans,
For the Yonghy-Bonghy-Bò,
For the Yonghy-Bonghy-Bò.

THE POBBLE
WHO HAS NO TOES

I.

The Pobble who has no toes
Had once as many as we;
When they said, "Some day you may lose them all;" –
He replied, – "Fish diddle de-dee!"
And his Aunt Jobiska made him drink,
Lavender water tinged with pink,
For she said, "The World in general knows
There's nothing so good for a Pobble's toes!"

II.

The Pobble who has no toes,
Swam across the Bristol Channel;
But before he set out he wrapped his nose
In a piece of scarlet flannel.
For his Aunt Jobiska said, "No harm
Can come to his toes if his nose is warm;
And it's perfectly known that a Pobble's toes
Are safe, – provided he minds his nose."

III.

The Pobble swam fast and well,
And when boats and ships came near him
He tinkedly-binkedly-winkled a bell,
So that all the world could hear him.
And all the Sailors and Admirals cried,
When they saw him nearing the further side, –
"He has gone to fish, for his Aunt Jobiska's
Runcible Cat with crimson whiskers!"

IV.

But before he touched the shore,
The shore of the Bristol Channel,
A sea-green Porpoise carried away
His wrapper of scarlet flannel.
And when he came to observe his feet,
Formerly garnished with toes so neat,
His face at once became forlorn
On perceiving that all his toes were gone!

V.

And nobody ever knew
From that dark day to the present,
Whoso had taken the Pobble's toes,
In a manner so far from pleasant.
Whether the shrimps or crawfish gray,
Or crafty Mermaids stole them away –
Nobody knew; and nobody knows
How the Pobble was robbed of his twice five toes!

VI.

The Pobble who has no toes
Was placed in a friendly Bark,
And they rowed him back, and carried him up,
To his Aunt Jobiska's Park.
And she made him a feast at his earnest wish
Of eggs and buttercups fried with fish; –
And she said; – "It's a fact the whole world knows,
That Pobbles are happier without their toes."

THE
QUANGLE WANGLE'S
HAT

I.

On the top of the Crumpetty Tree
The Quangle Wangle sat,
But his face you could not see,
On account of his Beaver Hat.
For his Hat was a hundred and two feet wide,
With ribbons and bibbons on every side
And bells, and buttons, and loops, and lace,
So that nobody ever could see the face
Of the Quangle Wangle Quee.

II.

The Quangle Wangle said
To himself on the Crumpetty Tree, –
"Jam; and jelly; and bread;
Are the best of food for me!
But the longer I live on this Crumpetty Tree,
The plainer than ever it seems to me
That very few people come this way,
And that life on the whole is far from gay!"
Said the Quangle Wangle Quee.

III.

But there came to the Crumpetty Tree,
Mr. and Mrs. Canary;
And they said, – "Did ever you see
Any spot so charmingly airy?
May we build a nest on your lovely Hat?
Mr. Quangle Wangle, grant us that!
O please let us come and build a nest
Of whatever material suits you best,
Mr. Quangle Wangle Quee!"

IV.

And besides, to the Crumpetty Tree
Came the Stork, the Duck, and the Owl;
The Snail, and the Bumble-Bee,
The Frog, and the Fimble Fowl;
(The Fimble Fowl, with a Corkscrew leg;)

And all of them said, – "We humbly beg,
We may build our home on your lovely Hat, –
Mr. Quangle Wangle, grant us that!
Mr. Quangle Wangle Quee!"

V.

And the Golden Grouse came there,
And the Pobble who has no toes, –
And the small Olympian bear, –
And the Dong with a luminous nose.
And the Blue Baboon, who played the flute, –
And the Orient Calf from the Land of Tute, –
And the Attery Squash, and the Bisky Bat, –
All came and built on the lovely Hat
Of the Quangle Wangle Quee.

VI.

And the Quangle Wangle said
To himself on the Crumpetty Tree, –
"When all these creatures move
What a wonderful noise there'll be!"
And at night by the light of the Mulberry moon
They danced to the Flute of the Blue Baboon,
On the broad green leaves of the Crumpetty Tree,
And all were as happy as happy could be,
With the Quangle Wangle Quee.

118

THE
AKOND of SWAT

Who or why, or which, or *what*,
Is the Akond of SWAT?

Is he tall or short, or dark or fair?
Does he sit on a stool or a sofa or chair,
or SQUAT,
The Akond of Swat?

Is he wise or foolish, young or old?
Does he drink his soup and his coffee cold,
or HOT,
The Akond of Swat?

Does he sing or whistle, jabber or talk,
And when riding abroad does he gallop or walk,
or TROT,
The Akond of Swat?

Does he wear a turban, a fez, or a hat?
Does he sleep on a mattress, a bed, or a mat,
or a COT,
The Akond of Swat?

When he writes a copy in a round-hand size,
Does he cross his t's and finish his i's
with a DOT,
The Akond of Swat?

Can he write a letter concisely clear
Without a speck or a smudge or smear
or BLOT,
The Akond of Swat?

Do his people like him extremely well?
Or do they, whenever they can, rebel,
or PLOT,
At the Akond of Swat?

If he catches them then, either old or young,
Does he have them chopped in pieces or hung,
or *shot*,
The Akond of Swat?

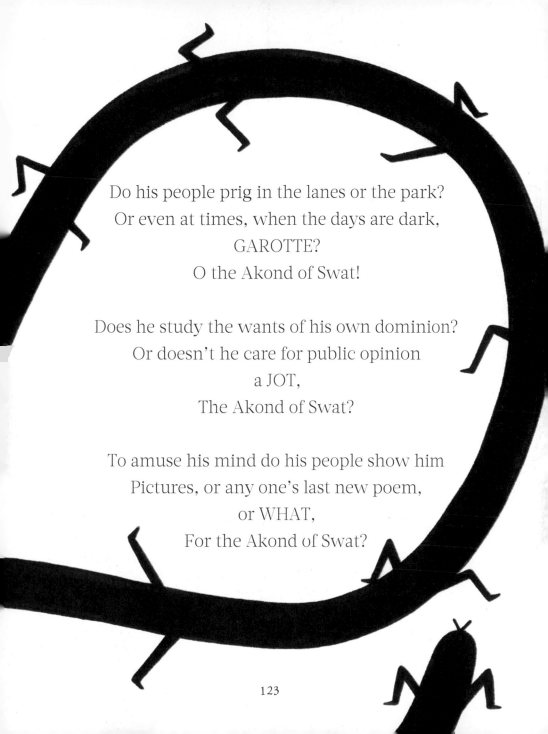

Do his people prig in the lanes or the park?
Or even at times, when the days are dark,
GAROTTE?
O the Akond of Swat!

Does he study the wants of his own dominion?
Or doesn't he care for public opinion
a JOT,
The Akond of Swat?

To amuse his mind do his people show him
Pictures, or any one's last new poem,
or WHAT,
For the Akond of Swat?

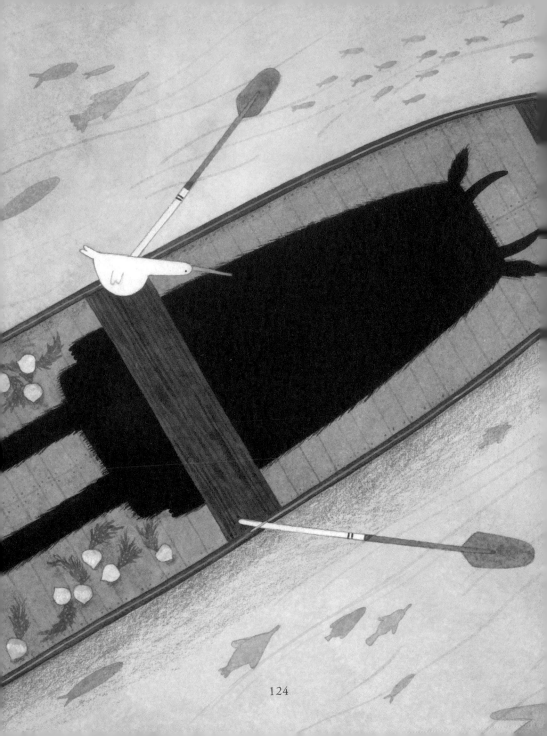

At night if he suddenly screams and wakes,
Do they bring him only a few small cakes,
        or a LOT,
    For the Akond of Swat?

Does he live on turnips, tea, or tripe?
Does he like his shawl to be marked with a stripe,
        or a DOT,
    The Akond of Swat?

Does he like to lie on his back in a boat
Like the lady who lived in that isle remote,
        SHALLOTT,
    The Akond of Swat?

Is he quiet, or always making a fuss?
Is his steward a Swiss or a Swede or a Russ,
or a SCOT,
The Akond of Swat?

Does he like to sit by the calm blue wave?
Or to sleep and snore in a dark green cave,
or a GROTT,
The Akond of Swat?

Does he drink small beer from a silver jug?
Or a bowl? or a glass? or a cup? or a mug?
or a POT,
The Akond of Swat?

Does he beat his wife with a gold-topped pipe,
When she lets the gooseberries grow too ripe,
or ROT,
The Akond of Swat?

Does he wear a white tie when he dines with friends,
And tie it neat in a bow with ends,
or a KNOT,
The Akond of Swat?

Does he like new cream, and hate mince-pies?
When he looks at the sun does he wink his eyes,
or NOT,
The Akond of Swat?

Does he teach his subjects to roast and bake?
Does he sail about on an inland lake,
in a YACHT,
The Akond of Swat?

Some one, or nobody, knows, I wot,
Who or which or why or what
Is the Akond of Swat!

ALPHABET

I

A

a

A was once an apple-pie,
Pidy
Widy
Tidy
Pidy
Nice insidy
Apple-pie.

B

b

B was once a little bear,
Beary!
Wary!
Hairy!
Beary!
Taky cary!
Little Bear!

C c

C was once a little cake,
Caky
Baky
Maky
Caky
Taky Caky,
Little Cake.

D
d

D was once a little doll,
Dolly
Molly
Polly
Nolly
Nursy Dolly
Little Doll!

E

e

E was once a little eel,
Eely
Weely
Peely
Eely
Twirly, Tweely
Little Eel!

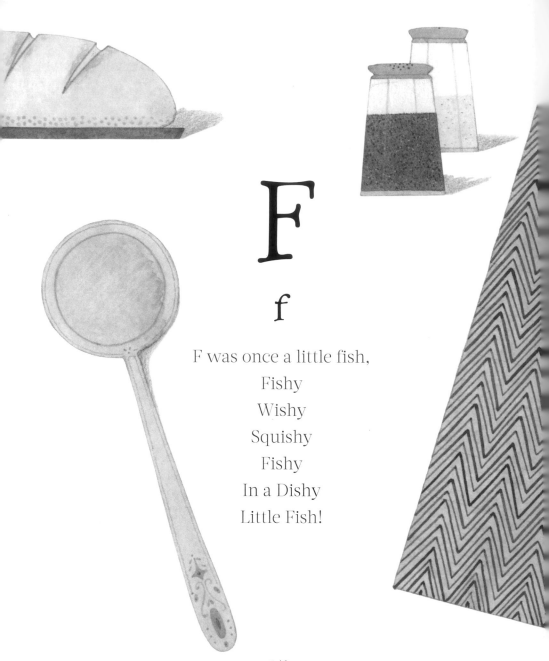

F
f

F was once a little fish,
Fishy
Wishy
Squishy
Fishy
In a Dishy
Little Fish!

G was once a little goose,
Goosy
Moosy
Boosey
Goosey
Waddly-woosy
Little Goose!

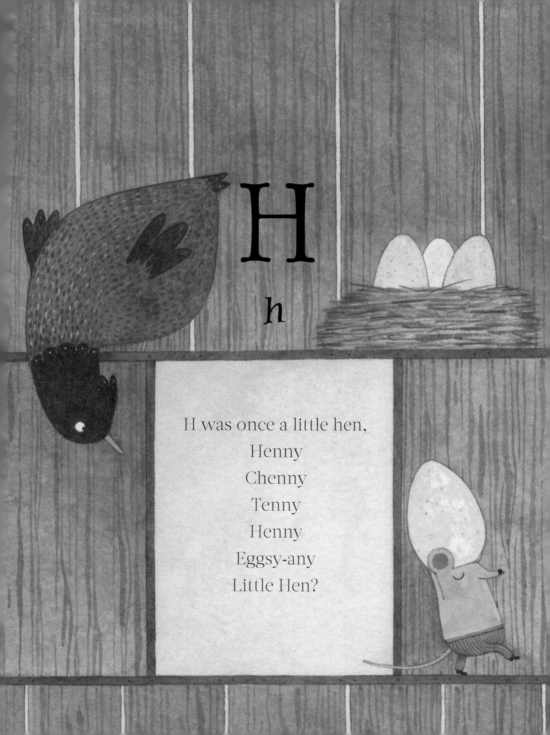

H
h

H was once a little hen,
Henny
Chenny
Tenny
Henny
Eggsy-any
Little Hen?

I
i

I was once a bottle of ink,
Inky
Dinky
Thinky
Inky
Blacky Minky
Bottle of Ink!

J
j

J was once a jar of jam,
Jammy
Mammy
Clammy
Jammy
Sweety – Swammy,
Jar of Jam!

K
k

K was once a little kite,
Kity
Whity
Flighty
Kity
Out of Sighty –
Little Kite!

L
l

L was once a little lark,
Larky!
Marky!
Harky!
Larky!
In the Parky,
Little Lark!

M m

M was once a little mouse,
Mousy
Bousey
Sousy
Mousy
In the Housy
Little Mouse!

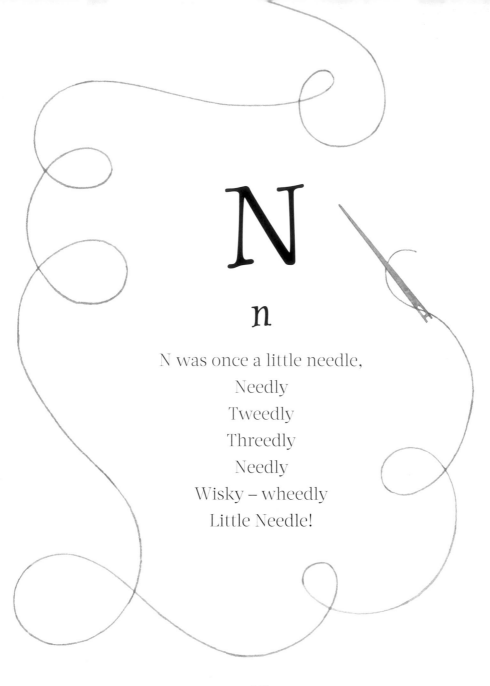

N
n

N was once a little needle,
Needly
Tweedly
Threedly
Needly
Wisky – wheedly
Little Needle!

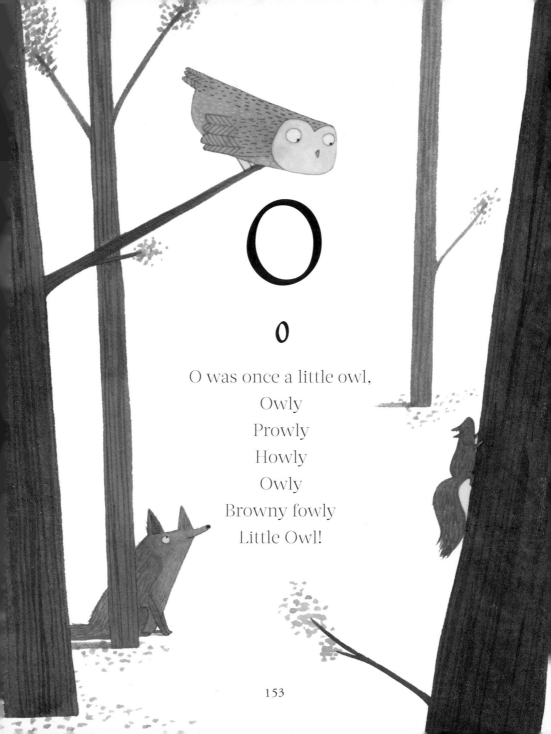

O

o

O was once a little owl,
Owly
Prowly
Howly
Owly
Browny fowly
Little Owl!

P

p

P was once a little pump,
Pumpy
Slumpy
Flumpy
Pumpy
Dumpy, Thumpy
Little Pump!

Q

q

Q was once a little quail,
Quaily
Faily
Daily
Quaily
Stumpy-taily
Little Quail!

R
r

R was once a little rose,
Rosy
Posy
Nosy
Rosy
Blows-y – grows-y
Little Rose!

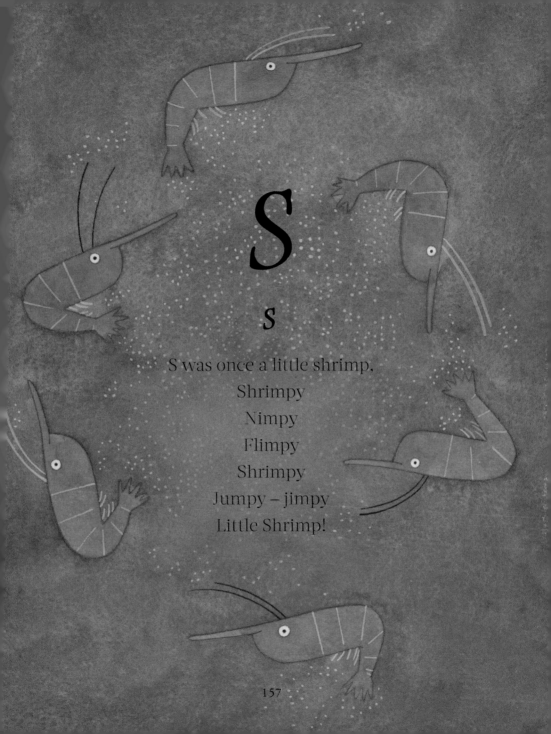

S
s

S was once a little shrimp,
Shrimpy
Nimpy
Flimpy
Shrimpy
Jumpy – jimpy
Little Shrimp!

T
t

T was once a little thrush,
Thrushy!
Hushy!
Bushy!
Thrushy!
Flitty – Flushy
Little Thrush!

U was once a little urn,
Urny
Burny
Turny
Urny
Bubbly – burny,
Little Urn.

V
v

V was once a little vine,
Viny
Winy
Twiny
Viny
Twisty-twiny
Little Vine!

W w

W was once a whale,
Whaly
Scaly
Shaly
Whaly
Tumbly-taily
Mighty whale!

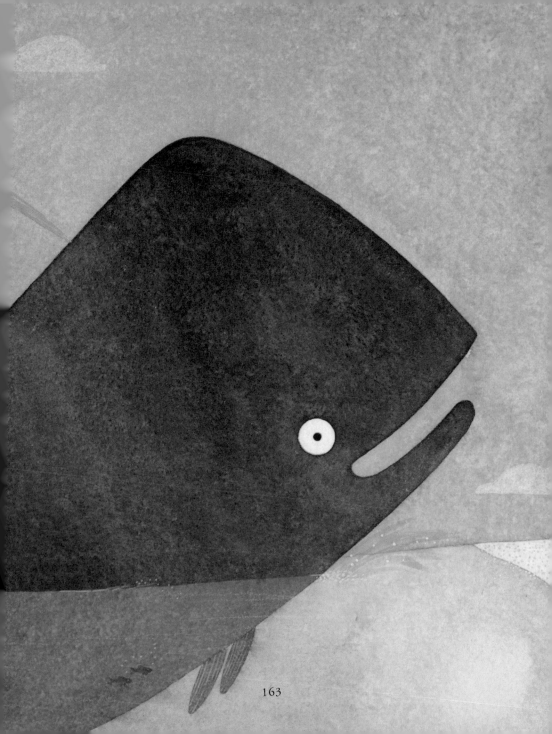

X

X

X was once a great king Xerxes,
Xerxy
Perxy
Turxy
Xerxy
Linxy Lurxy
Great King Xerxes!

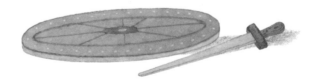

Y
y

Y was once a little yew,
Yewdy
Fewdy
Crudy
Yewdy
Growdy, grewdy,
Little Yew!

Z
z

Z was once a piece of zinc,
Tinky
Winky
Blinky
Tinky
Tinkly Minky
Piece of Zinc!

NONSENSE
BOTANY

COCKATOOCA
SUPERBA

FISHIA MARINA

THE FORK TREE

This pleasing and amazing Tree never grows above four hundred and sixty-three feet in height, — nor has any specimen hitherto produced above forty thousand silver forks at one time. If violently shaken it is most probable that many forks would fall off, — and in a high wind it is highly possible that all the forks would rattle dreadfully, and produce a musical tinkling to the ears of the happy beholder.

BOTTLEPHORKIA
SPOONIFOLIA

GUITTARA PENSILIS

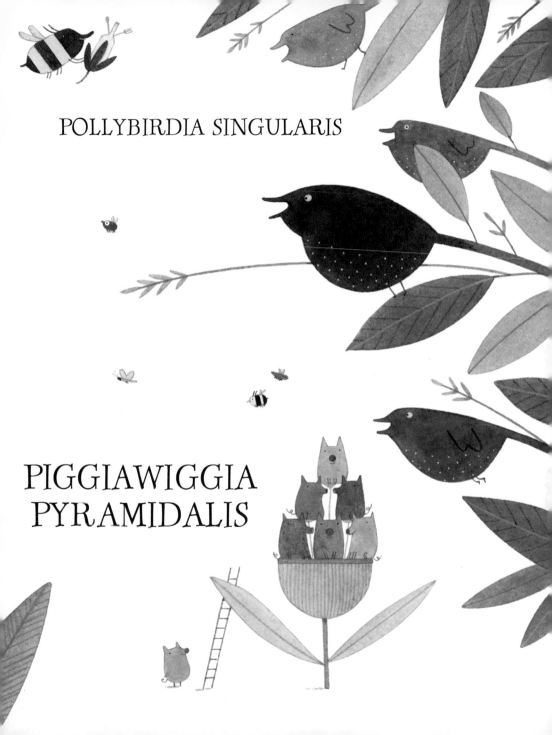

POLLYBIRDIA SINGULARIS

PIGGIAWIGGIA
PYRAMIDALIS

THE BISCUIT TREE

This remarkable vegetable production has never yet been described or delineated. As it never grows near rivers, nor near the sea, nor near mountains or vallies, or houses, — its native place is wholly uncertain. When the flowers fall off, and the tree breaks out in biscuits, the effect is by no means disagreeable, especially to the hungry. — If the Biscuits grow in pairs, they do not grow single, and if they ever fall off, they cannot be said to remain on.

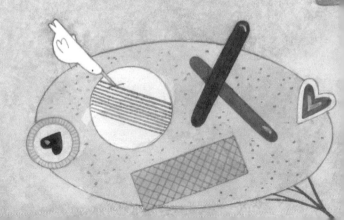

THE RABBIT
TREE

MANYPEEPLIAUPSIDOWNIA

PLUMBUNNIA
NUTRITIOSA

PHATFACIA STUPENDA

JINGLIA
TINKETTLIA

HOWOOOOOO
HOWOOOOOO
HOWOOOOOO

ENKOOPIA
CHICKABIDDIA

MINSPYSIA
DELICIOSA

ARTHBROOMIA
RIGIDA

THE CLOTHES-BRUSH TREE

This most useful natural production does not produce many clothes-brushes, which accounts for those objects being expensive.
The omsquombious nature of this extraordinary vegetable it is of course unnecessary to be diffuse upon.

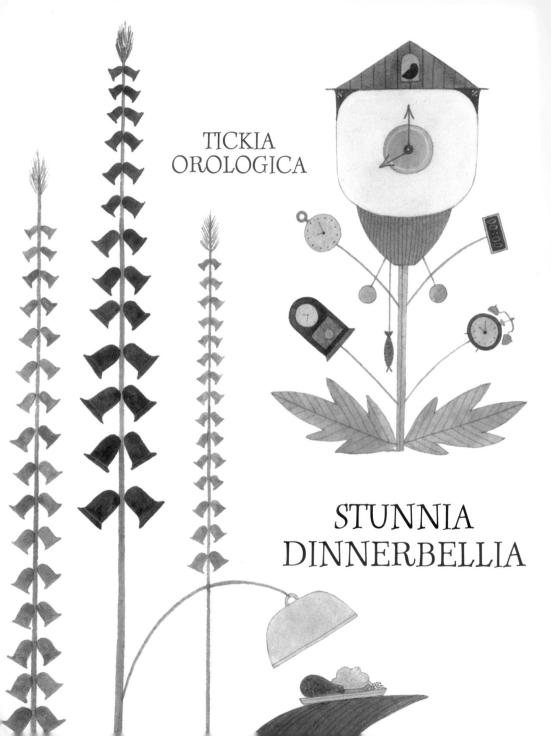

TICKIA
OROLOGICA

STUNNIA
DINNERBELLIA

SHOEBOOTIA UTILIS

SOPHTSLUGGIA
GLUTINOSA

THE DISH TREE

TIGERLILLIA
TERRIBILIS

WASHTUBBIA
CIRCULARIS

ARMCHAIRIA
COMFORTABILIS

BASSIA PALEALENSIS

BUBBLIA
BLOWPIPIA

BLUEBOTTLIA
BUZZTILENTIA

187

THE CLOMJOMBIMBILIOUS TREE

KNUTMIGRATA
SIMPLICE

TUREENIA
LADLECUM

189

THE KITE TREE

The Kite tree is a fearful and astonishing
vegetable when all the Kites are agitated by
a tremendous wind, and endeavour to
escape from their strings. The tree does not
appear to be of any particular use to society,
but would be frequented by small boys if
they knew where it grew.

PUFFIA
LEATHERBELLOWSA

SMALLTOOTHCOMBIA DOMESTICA

QUEERIFLORA BABYÖIDES

CRABBIA HORRIDA

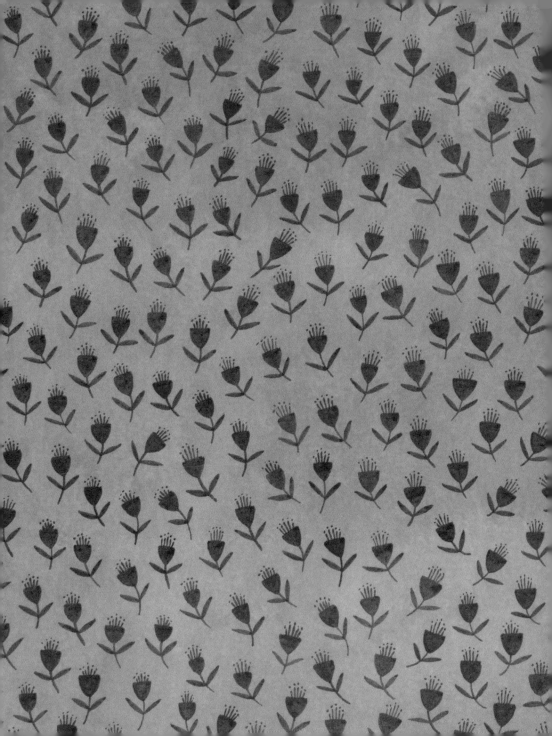

ALPHABET II

A

A was an ape,
Who stole some white tape
And tied up his toes
In four beautiful bows.
a!
Funny old Ape!

B

B was a bat,
Who slept all the day,
And fluttered about,
When the sun went away.
b!
Brown little bat!

C

C was a camel,
You rode on his hump,
And if you fell off,
You come down such a bump!
c!
What a high Camel!

D

D was a dove
Who lived in a wood
With such pretty soft wings,
And so gentle and good.
d!
Dear little Dove!

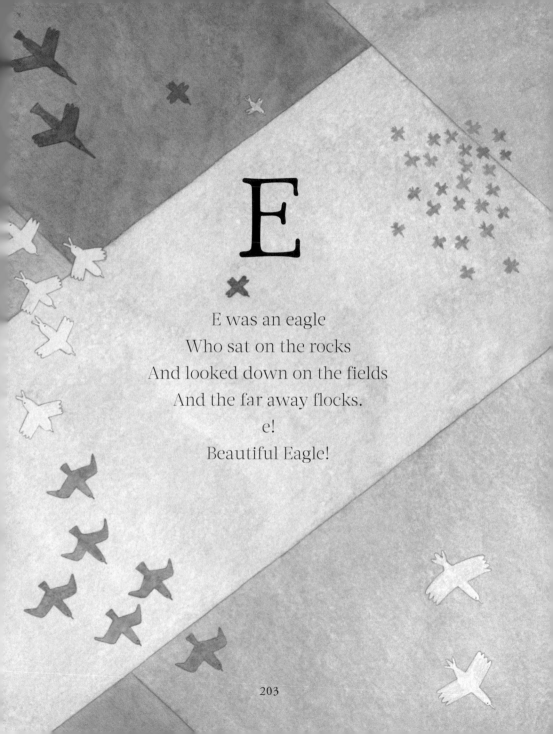

E

E was an eagle
Who sat on the rocks
And looked down on the fields
And the far away flocks.
e!
Beautiful Eagle!

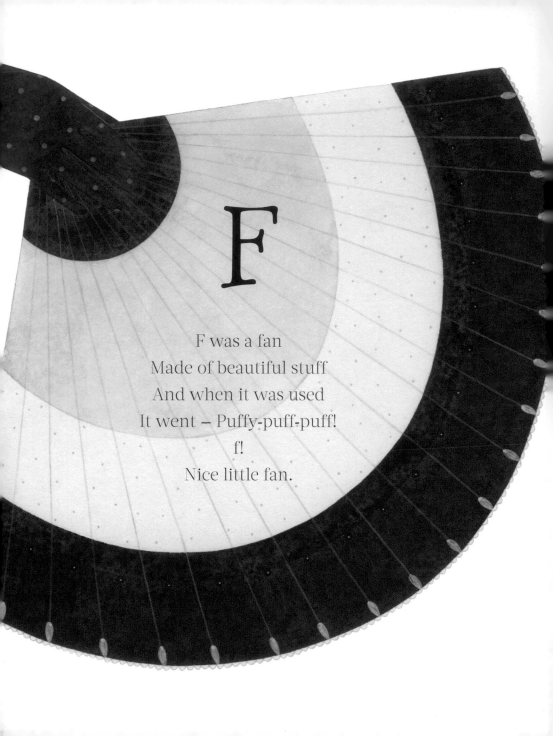

F

F was a fan
Made of beautiful stuff
And when it was used
It went — Puffy-puff-puff!
f!
Nice little fan.

G

G was a gooseberry
Perfectly red;
To be made into jam
And eaten with bread.
g!
Gooseberry red!

H

H was a heron
Who stood in a stream
The length of his neck
And his legs, was extreme!
h!
Long-legged Heron!

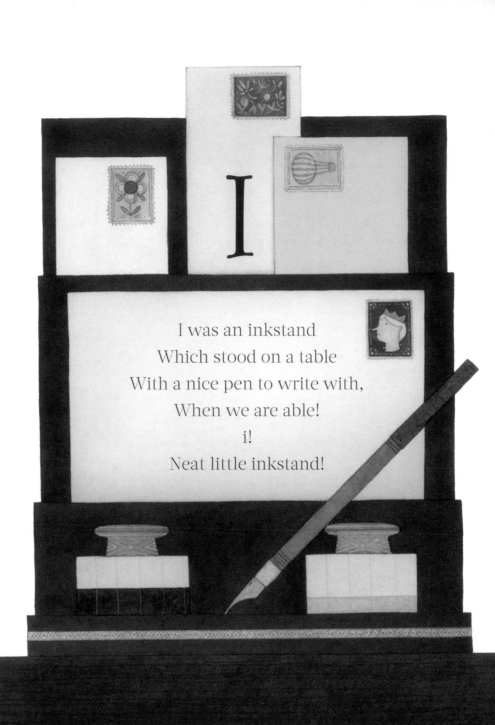

I was an inkstand
Which stood on a table
With a nice pen to write with,
When we are able!
i!
Neat little inkstand!

J was a jug,
So pretty and white
With fresh water in it
At morning and night.
j!
Nice little jug!

K

K was a kingfisher,
Quickly he flew
So bright and so pretty,
Green, purple, and blue.
k!
Kingfisher, blue!

211

L

L was a lily
So white and so sweet
To see it and smell it
Was quite a nice treat!
l!
Beautiful Lily

M

M was a man,
Who walked round and round,
And he wore a long coat
That came down to the ground.
m!
Funny old Man!

N

N was a nut
So smooth and so brown,
And when it was ripe
It fell tumble-dum-down.
n!
Nice little Nut!

O

O was an oyster
Who lived in his shell
If you let him alone
He felt perfectly well.
o!
Open mouth'd Oyster!

217

P

P was a polly
All red, blue and green,
The most beautiful polly
That ever was seen.
p!
Poor little Polly!

Q was a quill
Made into a pen,
But I do not know where
And I cannot say when.
q!
Nice little Quill!

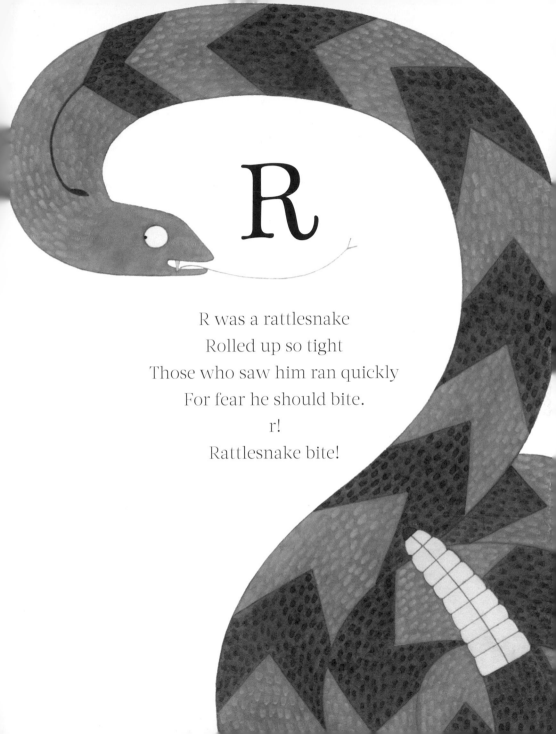

R

R was a rattlesnake
Rolled up so tight
Those who saw him ran quickly
For fear he should bite.
r!
Rattlesnake bite!

S was a screw
To screw down a box
And then it was fastened
Without any locks.
s!
Valuable screw!

T

T was a thimble
Of silver so bright
When placed on the finger
It fitted so tight!
t!
Nice little thimble!

U

U was an upper-coat
Woolly and warm
To wear over all
In the snow or the storm.
u!
What a nice upper-coat!

V

V was a veil
With a border upon it
And a riband to tie it
All round a pink bonnet.
v!
Pretty green Veil!

W

W was a watch
Where in letters of gold
The hour of the day
You might always behold.
w!
Beautiful watch!

X

X was King Xerxes
Who wore on his head
A mighty large turban,
Green, yellow, and red.
x!
Look at King Xerxes!

Y

Y was a yak
From the land of Thibet,
Except his white tail
He was all black as jet.
y!
Look at the Yak!

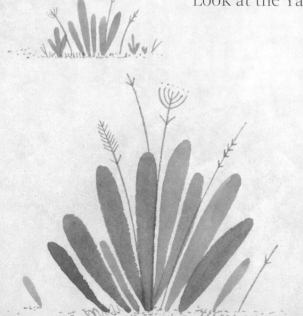

Z

Z was a zebra,
All striped white and black,
And if he were tame
You might ride on his back.
z!
Pretty striped Zebra!

EDWARD LEAR

A drawing of Edward Lear by the artist William Holman Hunt

Edward Lear was born in London, England, on 12th May, 1812. His parents, Jeremiah and Ann Lear, had twenty-one children – Edward was the twentieth! When he was five years old, his family lost most of their money, so he was sent to live with his eldest sister Ann, who was twenty-one years older than he was.

Edward suffered many health problems, including epilepsy, bronchitis and depression, which made him feel different from other children, and often lonely. His sister introduced him to art and poetry to keep him occupied, and it wasn't long before he discovered his own talents. Aged only fifteen, he sold some of his drawings, and was soon earning a living as an artist. He painted landscapes for the British Museum, and scientific illustrations of birds for the Zoological Society, which had just opened in Regent's Park, London.

As an adult, Lear toured many countries including Italy, Greece, Egypt and India, and painted the landscapes and wildlife he saw. His first book, *Illustrations of the Family of Psittacidae, or Parrots*, was published when he was only nineteen. One species of parrot he drew in Brazil was later named Lear's Macaw after him. The landscapes he painted were also published in books, and he became so well-known as an artist that he even gave drawing lessons to Queen Victoria.

The Earl of Derby commissioned him to draw the animals in his large menagerie at Knowsley Hall in Lancashire. Lear was very happy there, and enjoyed making up funny poems with drawings, to entertain the Earl's grandchildren. In 1846, some of these were published in *A Book of Nonsense*. He used the pen name, Derry Down Derry, because this book was so different from his others, and he didn't want to damage his reputation as a serious artist. It contained rhyming poems, each with only five lines. Lear called them 'nonsense, pure and absolute', because they were meant to be silly. We now call them limericks, but that name was not used until after Lear's death, and no one is quite sure where it comes from. Lear hadn't invented the style – it had been around for at least a few hundred years before him – but he made it popular.

Victorian society was very formal, and Victorian children's books mostly told children how they should behave. So this kind of nonsense literature offered welcome comic relief. Other writers of nonsense literature at the time included Lewis Carroll, who wrote *Alice's Adventures in Wonderland*. Lear wrote further books under his real name, containing limericks, nonsense botany, nonsense cookery, and nonsense songs, which were his longer poems. They were filled with invented characters such as the Jumblies and the Quangle Wangle, and made-up words, such as 'runcible' and 'crumpetty', which sounded interesting, but had no real meaning.

Later in life, Lear settled in San Remo, Italy, where he lived with his beloved cat, Foss. He died there in 1888, aged seventy-five.

USBORNE QUICKLINKS

For links to websites where you can find out more about Edward Lear, go to the Usborne Quicklinks website at **www.usborne.com/quicklinks** and type in the keywords "Edward Lear".

Here are some of the things you can do at the recommended websites:

* See inside a 19th century copy of *A Book of Nonsense*, with drawings by Edward Lear

* Watch a slideshow of Lear's landscape paintings

* Have a look at the diaries Lear wrote on his travels

ACKNOWLEDGEMENTS

Designed by Lucy Wain
Editor: Fiona Patchett

Managing Designer: Nicola Butler
Digital manipulation by Nick Wakeford and John Russell

Every effort has been made to trace the copyright holders of material in this book. If any rights have been omitted, the publishers offer to rectify this in any subsequent editions following notification.

p.236 © Walker Art Gallery, National Museums Liverpool/Bridgeman